ALSO BY HENRY ALFORD

Big Kiss: One Actor's Desperate Attempt to Claw His Way to the Top

Municipal Bondage: One Man's Anxiety-Producing Adventures in the Big City

Out There

HENRY ALFORD

OUT THERE

One Man's Search for the

Funniest Person on the Internet

NEW YORK

As of press time, the URLs displayed in the text of *Out There* link or refer to existing websites on the Internet. Random House, Inc., is not responsible for the content available on any such site (including, without limitation, outdated, inaccurate, or incomplete information), and access to any such site is at the user's own risk.

Copyright © 2001 by Henry Alford

All rights reserved under International and Pan-American Copyright Conventions. Published in the United States by Random House, Inc., New York, and simultaneously in Canada by Random House of Canada Limited, Toronto.

ATRANDOM.COM BOOKS and colophon are registered trademarks of Random House, Inc.

Grateful acknowledgment is made to the following for permission to reprint previously published material: ASTOR WOOD PRODUCTIONS: JaysKids.com claims are reprinted with permission of Astor Wood Productions and JaysKids.com. Trademark and copyright © 2000 by Astor Wood Productions. All rights reserved. Reprinted by permission. JEWS FOR THE PRESERVATION OF FIREARMS OWNERSHIP: Excerpts from the "Ask the Rabbi" column on the Jews for the Preservation of Firearms Ownership website (www.jpfo.org). Used by permission. KEVIN FOX, FURY.COM: AOLiza dialogues are copyright © Kevin Fox, Fury.com. Reprinted by permission. US MUSIC VAULT ONLINE: Matt Portenoy's reviews are copyright © The US Music Vault Online—www.usmusicvault.com. Reprinted by permission.

Library of Congress Cataloging-in-Publication Data

Alford, Henry.

Out there: one man's search for the funniest person on the Internet / Henry Alford.

p. cm.

ISBN 0-8129-9151-6 (pbk.)

1. Internet—Humor. I. Title.

PN6231.I62 A43 2001

004.67′802′07—dc21   2001022096

Website address: www.atrandom.com

Printed in the United States on acid-free paper

2 4 6 8 9 7 5 3

First Edition

FOR JONATHAN YARDLEY

Contents

I	Nonconfrontational Bitch on the Bus	1
II	I Have Always Felt the Voodoo Jive Is in Myself!	11
III	You Are a Very Small Pebble Impeding Our March Toward the Preservation of Our American Freedoms	21
IV	Flamma Lamma Ding Dong	43
V	Once, He Performed His Unusual Skill in a Restaurant, Startling a Waitress	61
VI	Many Womens Are Tickled Them Nose by Kleenex and Sneeze. Please Enjoy!	71
VII	I Could Do the Same Experiment with My Dog	87

PART I

NONCONFRONTATIONAL BITCH ON THE BUS

Chapter 1
—

It is commonly said—but I believe it anyway—that the Internet is glutted with individuals who produce an unceasing and meaningless din: crackpots who are madly typ-typ-typing into the night, keyboard commanders run amok.

This is true. The Internet is thick with people who regularly blur the line between writing and spamming.

But buried diamondlike within this whorl of wire are the rare exceptions: a handful of people who distinguish themselves by the originality of their vision and by the zeal with which they hurl it into cyberspace.

I'm talking about people like the Frenchman, now living in southern California, who captions the erotic photoplays on his website in a misspelled and mangled English, producing gems of dialogue such as

A little enthousiasm could do marvel around here!

I'm talking about people like the Michigan bed-and-breakfast owner whose ad assures us,

Everything is garnished.

I'm talking about people like the movie reviewer on a Christian site whose review of the *South Park* movie catalogues various "examples of ignominy in this celluloid developed in the fiery pits of hell," including the scene in which "an all-male chorus line wore pink bikini briefs," and the fact that the Lord's name was taken in vain seventeen times, and, perhaps most upsetting, that

Angels were portrayed as nude—very nude—females.

Chapter 2

If you want to avail yourself of a strange vantage point on American culture, you could do worse than to turn to the site Anger Central [www.angry.net]. Anger Central is a collection of shortish screeds and diatribes sent in by random plaintiffs and organized alphabetically by topic.

Here is invective, regularly spaced. Here are troubled minds unburdened by tact or grammar (these troubled minds are nude—very nude).

Sometimes, when I am having a kind of slow day—one of those days when I find myself devoting a loosely measured amount of time to determining my body weight on Mars (60.3 pounds)—I will scroll through Anger Central and see what people are angry about. I'll while away an hour or so, intrigued by the fact that people get just as worked up over very tiny sources of outrage (e.g., potted meats) as they do over large ones (e.g., the Catholic Church). Under the category "Things," for instance, I'll find rants with titles such as

> Being black
> Being laid off
> Cable company, Tucson
> ducks
> Hiroshima bomb
> irony
> MORALS
> Nuts and Raisins
> Vomiting
> Yard sales
> Zippers

And then I'll buzz through some of the listings under the heading "People," intrigued by what I find there:

> BITCH
> Two faced Back Stabbing Bitch
> Non-confrontational bitch on the bus
> Bitch sister in law
> Happy Bubbly Bitch
> KB the thieving bitch
> lying sons of bitches
> Marla the BITCH
> Paranoid bitch
> PREDATORY BITCHES
> Sasquatch Bitch
> Rehab Bitch
> Jeremy Bentham
> Ayn Rand
> Iowa Septuplets
> You

While reading the rants themselves can soon enough go stale—a lot of these people *wish* they could get on afternoon television—imagining what kind of person wrote each one is reliably involving.

Also, I find I have questions. Did the person who wrote the rant entitled "my cousin the navel flaunter" also write "needy masseuse"? And in the self-interested, nonutilitarian stance taken by the person who posted "Jeremy Bentham," do I detect the literary stylings of "Happy Bubbly Bitch" herself?

As it turns out, my questions will never be answered: all the posts on Anger Central are unsigned.

Indeed, the Internet often poses the question of authorship. Sometimes the item in question is unsigned; other times it has more than one author—such as the unnamed graduate students who write Plotbyte's dumbed-down answer to Cliffs Notes [www.schoolbytes.com], like this one for *Wuthering Heights:*

> Nobody knows how Emily Bronte wrote all this because she was really reclusive and never really dated or had any friends. This book is so confusing because everyone is somehow related to everyone else. It is like a backwoods trailer community. You know, where everybody is "cousins."

But usually the reason why we don't know the identity of the person we're reading on the Web is, of course, a function of the medium itself: the anonymity of being online precludes our knowing. On the Internet, most of us use a "handle" that is not our own name.

Moreover, some people, under the guise of their handle, are pretending to be someone they're not. One of the first lessons we learn when we go online is this: the presence in a chat room of more than one person identifying himself as a "teenage lesbian" is a strong if not certain indication that, in fact, there are *no* teenage lesbians currently chatting there.

But this tradition of dissembling points up an essential aspect of online culture: anyone who has ever worn a Halloween mask or made a prank phone call knows that, with your actual identity masked, you can—and sometimes will—do things that you otherwise might not. You're more daring, more likely to utter "Cowabunga!," more likely to lead a fully-clothed conga line into the swimming pool of the unknown.

Granted, people operating under false identities occupy a small portion of Web traffic. But I submit that the oftentimes raw quality of what we encounter online owes something to this lowering of accountability. Left alone in his parents' house while they are away, man cooks up a slightly exaggerated version of himself.

—

The Internet has opened a floodgate. About a year ago I noticed that whenever the people in my life needed to convey a message forged in passion—a rebuke to a slight I had dealt them, the recounting of something that had made them laugh, the unveiling of amorous feelings—they tended to e-mail me rather than write a letter or call me or tell me in person.

Increasingly, I pursue this line of action, too. If I had to, say, chastise you—and let me simply state right here, Reader, that as of page 8, I am already feeling a *lot* of hostility toward you—I would be tempted to convey this criticism electronically.

Why?

For several reasons.

First, of course, I hate it when you yell in my ear.

Second, when I communicate with you electronically, I am not Henry Alford, an actual breathing freelance writer who lives in New York City, where he tries to reconcile the gap between precipitously steep mortgage payments and the writing of "humorous" volumes yielding less-than-Grisham sales. No, I am Hankalf, an abstraction. No, I am Hankalf—carefree, frisky, unmortgaged: a scamp!

Third, the medium itself is the ultimate in McLuhanesque cool; if face-to-face communications are the most direct route at my disposal, then screen-to-screen ones are the most remote. From the stronghold of this remoteness, I will rocket at you my poisoned arrow.

If a lowering of accountability removes the filters from our e-mails by allowing us to present ourselves to the world with fewer restrictions, then the concept that media critics call "disintermediation" opens the valve of websites and Web commerce. Disintermediation is the removal of middle management—editors, publishers, agents, brokers, copy editors—who have historically acted as intermediaries between writers/producers and their readers/consumers. (The economic ramifications of this movement, of course, are huge. I pity the travel agents and small-bookstore owners and merchants who grow less relevant in the face of the techno-behemoth; in the future, only the very, very rich or the very, very poor will ever lay eyes on a human member of the service industry.)

Disintermediation is both a blessing and a curse. A blessing because more people are given an opportunity to showcase their goods in the marketplace; a curse because many of these goods are starting to attract fruit flies.

———

But, on the whole, fewer restrictions mean more opportunity.

For this, I—reader, malingerer—am grateful.

Because now a fan of the actor Klaus Kinski will go to the message board of a site for Kinski fans and express his disappointment over one of the actor's career choices by writing:

> I am a malcontented lickspittle!

Because now a Dunkin' Donuts patron will go to a site for Dunkin' Donuts patrons and write:

> I have always been very potent in the bedroom, until a Dunkin Donuts store opened near my home. I was tempted by their Bavarian cream donut and began eating several a day. At the same time, I began having difficulty getting and sustaining an erection. After several weeks of impotence, I made what I believe to be a connection between my donut consumption and my sexual disorder. I immediately stopped eating the donuts,

and within three days I found I was back to my usual virile self. I cannot be sure, but the possibility that Dunkin Donuts caused this problem leads me to believe that research needs to be completed and caution must be taken.

This donut confession is poetry; it's Whitman the donut eater. I can't not read such poetry; stumbling across it in cyberspace fills me with the same sensation that I get when, as a consumer, I confront merchandise that I don't particularly need, but that is hugely reduced in price.

Indeed, websites can be like merchandise outlets: places, located along the information superhighway, for the unloading on a gullible public of goods of questionable provenance or dubious quality.

Yes, a site can be very much like a carpet warehouse of someone's mind.

PART II

I HAVE ALWAYS FELT THE VOODOO JIVE IS IN MYSELF!

Chapter 3

—

And so I surf.

I sift, I pan for gold.

Sometimes I wonder, Why am I so intensely drawn to this alternate universe? Why, for that matter, is anyone?

Mark Slouka, who wrote *War of the Worlds: Cyberspace and the Hi-Tech Assault on Reality,* told *Harper's* that "the wired world is a response to certain cultural changes over the last two or three generations—the breakup of the family, the breakdown of the community, the degradation of the physical environment.... As we observe this assault on the physical world, we feel ourselves losing control. I think alternative worlds become more appealing to us."

All of which I heartily agree with. In fact, one of the most interesting and oddly moving sites on the Web confronts at least one of these issues—the breakup of the family—head on. Below are posts written by seven people on Jayskids.com [www.jayskids.com], a site started to track down the children of deceased blues singer

Screamin' Jay Hawkins, who claimed to have fathered fifty-seven children.

> I'm his lovechild. I sing just like him. I look very similar also, in an Irish American kind of way.
>
> My mother was an English teacher running around the world, I'm the singer in a band, I practice voodoo, I'm constipated and bluesy every day.
>
> When I was twelve years old, I was sitting at a truck stop in suburban New Jersey with my mother. I asked her what flavor ice cream she wanted, and she said, "You are the child of the famed rhythm and blues artist Screamin' Jay Hawkins." From that moment on, I knew I was marked for greatness.
>
> I think he's my poppa and that I was put up for adoption and given to the parents I have now. You see, I am very creative. I write, act, sing, and produce and none of my parents do this. They work in industrial factories.
>
> I have always felt the voodoo jive is in myself! It is an innate urge. Where else does one get it?
>
> My mom has pictures of him and I don't have a dad. Please help me.
>
> I don't want to be found. I know I am one of his kids. I just want my family and friends to know I'm all right and I have a great life now.

And when the Web is *not* directly addressing the large forces of cultural change that are rending the fabric of our country asunder—which is to say, 99.9 percent of the time—it is still able to provide sustenance in a mysterious way.

Indeed, many and ineffable are the benefits to be had from visiting the bulletin board of a website for fans of Charlton Heston and reading:

> Chuck is the greatest, but that animal sitting on top of his head has got to go. Chuck, you must have enough money to buy a quality hair-piece.

Chapter 4

Then one day, it came from out of the blue: my friend (and editor) Jon suggested to me that I search for the funniest person on the Internet.

Here was an opportunity to shine additional light on semi-obscured talent; here was an opportunity to designate a group of strangers whom I could refer to as "my people." I had always felt that the voodoo jive was in *myself;* but now I could look for it in others, too.

I decided to take the plunge.

How to proceed, though? My methodology was as follows. First, I told everyone I know about my search; this part of the campaign took the form of e-mails, phone calls, and quiet dinners involving liquor.

Then, I told as many people I *don't* know as possible. I effected this latter part of the campaign by posting a bulletin on Abuzz [www.abuzz.com] and then by mentioning my search in several contributor's notes in magazines (*The New Yorker, eCompany Now,* and *Travel & Leisure*), one of which caught the eye of a reporter at *The Wall Street Journal,* to whom I gave an interview. I also talked about the project in an interview I gave to the online journal Ironminds [www.ironminds.com].

While the suggestions and submissions trickled in, I started my own combing, too, consulting a variety of printed and online sources. The most helpful of these were Scott Alexander's column "Weird Sites" on Yahoo's site [www.zdnet.com/yil]; back issues of *People, Harper's,* and *Yahoo Internet Life;* and a blog (short for "Web log," a site that describes and provides links to a variety of other sites) called Mister Pants [www.misterpants.com].

Even at this early point in the search, two things became immediately apparent to me. First, I was not particularly interested in tapping sources like *The Onion, McSweeney's,* or *Modern Humorist*—sites that are essentially humor magazines, usually written by professional humorists. This did not seem to be the best use of my skills. I had not, in my role as humorologist, donned a pith helmet in order to walk into my backyard to rhapsodize over my golden retriever, known to all; I was in search of the three-legged ibex.

Second, I prefer text to image. This, no doubt, has something to do with my own background and literary aspirations, but it also has something to do with you. Namely, I wanted you to be able to experience these folks on the page for yourself as much as possible; I didn't want to try to conjure up what their cartoon or movie looked like, worried, all along, that you might mistake the conjuring for the conjured. (And at the same time I did not want you to hyperlink away from my book to go look at someone else's work for long periods of time: I will brook no distractions from the blazing glory of my own shimmery and magisterial prose!)

Other than acknowledging these two prejudices, I imposed no constraints at the beginning of my search. The humor could be intentional or unintentional; its purveyor could be anonymous or known. Once I had unearthed all my contenders, then, yes, I would act as gatekeeper, determining which work was original and laugh-producing, and which work was simply stolen *Saturday Night Live* dialogue interspersed with fart jokes.

But here, at the beginning of my search, I simply wanted to amass.

I simply wanted to behold what loomed before me: the world's Open Mike Night.

PART III

YOU ARE A VERY SMALL PEBBLE IMPEDING OUR MARCH TOWARD THE PRESERVATION OF OUR AMERICAN FREEDOMS

Chapter 5

—

And so, eager to press my ear against the hot tar of the information superhighway, eager to offer myself up as arbiter and gatekeeper of the world's comedically inclined, I plumbed the offerings.

I viewed; I downloaded.

My first impression: this will be the filthiest book I ever write.

Yes, among the early submissions, the keynote was filth. Yet one individual stood out among the filthmongers.

Donna Anderson is a rock-and-roll groupie—actually, more a heavy-metal groupie—who writes a column on a site called Metal Sludge [www.metal-sludge.com/DonnasDomain.htm].

Miss Anderson has two gambits: she has compiled "The Long and Short of It," a field guide to the rock star penis; she also responds to the letters, many of them also manhood-driven in topic, that readers send in.

In order to create the vast encyclical that is "The Long and Short of It"—by column's end, the reader has little doubt that he is in the presence of the John James Audubon of the rock-and-roll schlong—

Anderson has culled information from a large network of information gatherers. This broad-based support no doubt gives the column its heft, its authority.

While "The Long and Short of It" displays a preoccupation with size of equipment—Anderson takes great pains to distinguish wee, preshrunk disappointment-makers from heavy-metal Jedis—its worldview is not wholly defined by this rather limited vantage point.

Art Alexakis of Everclear, Anderson tells us, "tries to come off as such a sincere, sweet guy but he's a HUGE slut"; John Lowery (Marilyn Manson/DLR Band) has specific notions about where to deposit the fruits of his excitement, and is enamored of the " 'pour wax on my dick' thing." Axl Rose apparently had one of his companions defecate in a box of kitty litter; Anderson responds by saying that she won't speak for all women, but as for herself, her own genitals "ain't going anywhere near" a cardboard box full of feline ordure.

Throughout the work, the reader is impressed by the fact that Anderson's wit never distracts from the acuity of her vision; one is put in mind of the young Kenneth Tynan.

Anderson displays her writerly hallmarks—pith and intense skepticism—in the letters section of her column, too.

In one letter, a young woman writes that when her mother was young, she once hung out with a rocker named Ryan Roxie at the Cat Club in New York City, and that Roxie tried to get her mother to perform fellatio on him. The writer adds that someone named Joe Leste of Bang Tango felt her up and that a fellow named Jizzy Pearl—this gal specializes in intense encounters with *very* obscure rock stars—kissed her after a show. She concludes her missive, "Sluts—all of them!" To which Anderson fires back:

> They weren't the only sluts.

Indeed, Anderson takes no prisoners; she is never afraid to alienate the person she is addressing. Some comic talents take their barbs right to the proverbial edge; others, like Anderson, take them to the edge of that edge.

Another music lover writes to Anderson in order to take the high road—it is possible, she writes, for girls to visit band members in their hotel room and not have sex "in any way." It depends on the individuals involved, she asserts; she herself has been in Sebastian Bach's hotel room, and "we just talked and watched 'The Bold and the Beautiful.' " She was once in Marty Friedman's room, too, and "nothing ever happened there either."

Anderson's reply is terse; could the reason the rockers remained decorous, she wonders, be

> because you weigh 250?

Besides her trenchant wit, what distinguishes Anderson from her filthmongering Internet brethren is that she is providing her readers with an, ahem, service. Yes, one could argue that *all* pornography has a practical application by virtue of its being fuel for fantasy. But Anderson's work is a call to action; it incites the reader to get out of his house. In short, it's News You Can Use.

I applaud this.

Also, Anderson's work has the ring of authenticity to it. The reader is led to feel that each of the rock stars in question has been thoroughly and professionally assessed. This level of professionalism—this kind of exhaustive, hands-on information gathering—is unmatched on most of the Web, save perhaps by the folks at Amish.Net [www.amish.net], who assure us that if a site visitor has a question about the Pennsylvania Dutch that is not already answered on the site, the webmaster will run the question by an actual Amish person.

Two other people on the Web who provide service bear mentioning. Grammar Lady [www.grammarlady.com] is a woman named Mary

Newton Bruder who answers readers' questions not only about grammar but about diction, syntax, and usage as well; it will probably not surprise you to learn that she "won't answer uncapitalized or unpunctuated messages."

While Grammar Lady usually strikes a tone of friendly, almost goofy fun—e.g., asking readers for "great tips" for activities in Italy, where she is visiting her backpacking daughter, or recounting a joke about a French art thief who, his van having run out of gas, says, "I had no Monet to buy Degas to make the Van Gogh"—she occasionally assumes an air of grammarian despair. Yes, there are dark clouds on the Grammar Lady horizon. Note, for instance, the evocation of doom in her response to one reader's query about whether "quote" can be used as a noun:

> Things have gotten very loose lately . . .

Grammar Lady's vision of a dystopian future is all too clear: in a garbage-strewn tenement, an exclamation point is holding a dangling participle at gunpoint; out in the street, flames erupt from an overturned gerund.

—

Equally as impassioned about his own cause is Rabbi R. Mermelstein, who writes an advice column called "Ask the Rabbi," on the Jews for the Preservation of Firearms Ownership site [www.jpfo.org/askrabbi.htm].

In addition to being ordained, Mermelstein is a former manufacturer of high-grade ammunition for rifles and handguns. He brings to his column the feisty zeal of both disciplines, but with a lotta heart, a lotta heart. When one reader asks if the rabbi knows of any Jewish shooting groups in South Florida, he responds,

> Legitimate firearms enthusiasts are one extended family regardless of their religious beliefs. When I'm around such folks

I'm usually in good company. Our hobby (passion?) transcends all religious and ethnic lines.

Another person asks the rabbi for recommendations for the beginning shooter. The rabbi responds,

> My standard advice to beginning handgun shooters is to cut your teeth on a .22 Long Rifle pistol or revolver. If rifles are your interest, the .22 Long Rifle is still my choice for the ability to practice to your heart's content on just a few dollars' worth of ammunition. Should you come to desire a longer-range rifle (beyond fifty yards), consider a bolt-action .223 Remington rifle. The Remington 700, in any one of its many permutations, is the pick of the litter from among production rifles. Top it off with a quality scope. More scopes of the variable power type, specifically the 3–9×, are sold than any other. Should you decide on a shotgun, the Remington 870 Police (18″ or 20″ barrel) can't be beat for quality and dollar value.
>
> Rabbi R. Mermelstein

Yes, there is much practical information to be had here, too. Wondering if 9-mm shells can be used in a .357 mag revolver? Need an inexpensive double-action semiauto pistol like a police return S&W 645, but not sure if the S&W 645 has a decocker feature? Ever wake up in the middle of the night wondering, "Why turn-bolt over semi-auto for long-range accuracy work?" The rabbi has answered all these questions.

The rabbi is sometimes asked to defend his stance. When one reader asks if there are places in the Talmud where the use of firearms is advocated, the rabbi responds that the Torah clearly advocates self-defense, and while a fire poker or pipe wrench might fit the bill,

> Firearms are more efficient.

28 · *Out There*

No one would ever accuse the rabbi of being mealymouthed.

This clarity of attack is winningly juxtaposed with the slightly unbridled nature of those who are drawn to the Mermelsteinian vision.

Rabbi:
First I wanna say that I'm French. When I read such a stupid page I think there's a lot of crazy guys in the world. The guns must be forbidden and you people jailed for encouraging gun ownership. I think you're this kind of dangerous people as the religious fanatical people.

Dear Sir:
This e-mail is hysterical, and your perception of history is pathetic. Twice in this century the U.S. has saved your people from speaking German and worshiping at the feet of a German demagogue. Your people, trying to curry favor with the Nazis, planted trees all along the streets of Paris because the Nazi troops were uncomfortable marching in the sun! We Americans saved you cowering sycophants with guns. And you have the peerless audacity to criticize firearms ownership? If you don't like our Web site, you may consider visiting Web sites about European socialism and Bordeaux wines. By the way, learn some better manners before you speak to a clergyman as you did in your e-mail.

Another letter.

QUESTION: What kind of Jews are you people anyhow????

Now as a peace-loving Jew I have heard of everything!! Are you people for real!!! The main problem besides religion in the world especially in the USA is firearms.
And you call yourself a Rabbi??????????????

H.S. Tapper
just a jew living in Canada, thank G-d

Mr. Tapper:
You are a loyal subject (read serf) of the British Crown, whose ungodly yoke we Americans, thank G-d, cast off over two centuries ago.
Do us Americans a favor, would you please? Occupy your hands and mandibles with your 4:00 p.m. tea and scones. You are a very small pebble impeding our march toward the preservation of our American freedoms. Your presence in Canada is a great comfort to us all.

Rabbi R. Mermelstein

The rabbi's work is not without historical import. Although somewhat obscure, the history of weapons-mongering by members of the Jewish faith can be seen to extend from the Old Testament to Henry Kissinger. The Jews for the Preservation of Firearms Ownership site's "Ask the Rabbi" column extends this tradition in a way that is both winning and highly unconventional, and thus one wonders how this legacy will manifest itself next.

My guess: Hadassah ladies who blow darts.

Chapter 6
—

The other form of service encountered frequently on the Web is, of course, criticism.

Popular music is a huge source of contention for Internet folk. Sometimes these music-inspired jeremiads occur where one does not expect to find them. When a visitor to jazz guitarist Pat Metheny's site [www.patmethenygroup.com] queried Metheny about musician Kenny G, Metheny took the opportunity to vent over a recent recording in which Kenny G overdubbed his own reed-blowing on top of Louis Armstrong's version of "What a Wonderful World."

Metheny writes that, in choosing to "defile" the work of the world's "greatest jazz musician" by "spewing his lame-ass, jive, pseudo-bluesy, out-of-tune, noodling, wimped out, fucked-up playing" over Armstrong's work, Kenny G "shit all over the graves of all the musicians past and present" who have devoted their lives to creating original music. In short, Kenny G has "reached a new low point in modern culture. We let this slide at our own peril."

You can't deny what fun it is to witness the bewilderment, if not the gall, that one luminary sets off in another. In his essay "The

Secret Life of James Thurber," the humorist describes the mounting sense of disquiet and unease that came over him when he read Salvador Dalí's memoirs. Thurber recounts young Dalí's exploits—kicking a playmate off a bridge, biting a sick bat, caressing a crutch, and covering himself with goat dung and aspic "that he might give off the true and noble odor of the ram." Thurber compares his own more average Columbus, Ohio, boyhood to Dalí's extravagances and escapades and comes to this conclusion: "Let me be the first to say that the naked truth about me is to the naked truth about Salvador Dalí as an old ukelele in the attic is to a piano in a tree, and I mean a piano with breasts." This is what Metheny has found in Kenny G's tree, too—a piano with breasts.

Most refreshing about Metheny's straight-from-the-horse's-mouth kind of music criticism is that it is devoid of the cant that we associate with professional music critics. Note the absence in Metheny's indictment of the terms "seminal," "hot licks," "ear candy," or "power ballad." This shows admirable restraint.

Matt Portenoy is similarly, uh, restrained. Portenoy is a seventeen-year-old who lives in a New York City suburb, whence he reviews music for US Music Vault Online [www.usmusicvault.com]; his reviews are notable for their tendency to veer from a discussion of the album at hand and spin into the world of Matt.

> Is there really any point in devoting a piece of serious music journalism to Chevelle? They have already stolen roughly an hour from my life, an hour which I could have used to go fishing, to enjoy nature, to paint, to write, to run, to slam my head with a mallet repeatedly, to paper cut my eyes or to bury myself alive . . .

he writes of the album *Point #1*. He then compiles a list of "Things I Would Rather Do Than Listening to Chevelle Again," which includes an activity that we have *all* contemplated—

Dive headfirst into Janet Reno's ass and set up a small sunglasses shanty inside.

But Portenoy distinguishes himself from other purveyors of nasty critical bile by occasionally being able to be amusing about something he likes. He loved, for instance, the eponymous debut album of U.S. Crush, a group that plays simple, four-chord power rock. Halfway through his very positive review of same, he writes:

> Did I mention that the band is absolutely unbelievable to jog to? Something about the adrenaline fueled bombast of U.S. Crush's melodies aligns perfectly with the pulse of a human in motion, and thus an almost parasitic relationship is formed.

And then, a few sentences later:

> "You Wanna Be a Star" is the perfect number to turn on when you're doing 70 in a 55 zone: a loud, bratty piece of protopunk which will make you forget any and all consequences of your actions. With their evident use as an energy supplement, it is easy to forget that U.S. Crush is also incredibly fun.

In one instance, when asked to review an album by the Hansonlike teenybopper group the Moffatts, who do a song called "Sayin' I [heart symbol] You," Portenoy recuses himself for reasons of bewilderment and hands the review over to his sister Allison, who "is eight years old, goes to elementary school, and has two hamsters." Allison weighs in in a fashion befitting her credentials ("It was pretty good"; "It had good lyrics and the songs were really good"; "I think that they're good"). At the end of the review, Allison bleats,

> I feel tired and sick and alone and embarrassed. Please don't print this review.

Chapter 7

But you don't have to be related by blood to become a critic on the Internet. Anyone can whine!

On Amazon.com, customers post reviews of items ranging from academic texts to patio furniture to Ella Fitzgerald CDs; this rousing chorus of opinion is composed of equal parts slurping delight and peevish frustration. The Grundig 960 Classic AM/FM shortwave radio inspires the put-down "a great shame on the Grundig name," while actress Tovah Feldshuh's performance in the 1999 drama *A Walk on the Moon* gives way to "The three most exciting words in show business are Tovah! Tovah! Tovah!"

A seemingly innocuous item such as Uncle Milton's Giant Ant Farm—one of those notebook-sized, clear-plastic housing units for real ants—becomes, on Amazon, a magnet for dissent. One customer calls it "an education in ignorance" and points out that ants can easily be viewed in a less artificial and cruel environment if you're simply willing to "get off your keister"; another customer opines that the toy is primarily a means for allowing children to ponder "the inescapability of their own mortality" (after about three weeks in their plastic home, this customer informs us, the ants enter their "death-pile phase").

The majority of these self-appointed critics publishing on Amazon strike a note of disappointment or regret; a desire to issue warning or grievance more strongly motivates a consumer to sit down and write a review than does a desire to exult in happy ownership. However, sometimes a book sold on Amazon unleashes in its readers feelings of magisterial critical acumen and gives way to an efflorescence of encomiastic critical writing.

Such is the case with *What Does This Say?*, a collection of "The Family Circus" cartoons by Bil Keane.

You remember "The Family Circus"—the circular, single-frame cartoon that features the adorable antics of Barfy the dog and his human playmates, PJ, Jeffy, and Billy, who sometimes express their incomprehension by uttering, "Ida know."

One *What Does This Say?* critic notes that the volume is Keane's most complex to date, stating that just at the moment when the reader feels like he understands the book's meaning, one of the work's more sophisticated arguments bonks him on the head like an anvil plummeting from high atop a forty-eight-story edifice "in the business district of a medium-sized city north of the Mason-Dixon line," forcing the reader first to feel pain and then to say the book's title aloud.

Indeed, this book seems to drop an anvil on each of its readers. Newark, New Jersey, resident MaidenFan claims that reading "The Family Circus" is highly reminiscent of listening to the heavy metal band Iron Maiden, "(who rulz!)." MaidenFan is particularly enamored of the "Family Circus" strips that run on Sundays, because they are often written in a "follow-the-trail" format wherein one of the children's tiny footsteps lead us from hilarious episode to hilarious episode; he even provides us with the names of specific Iron Maiden tunes that enhance this experience. (MaidenFan would probably have some effective marketing ideas for the Janet Reno sunglasses shanty, too.)

Another Keane fan enumerates all the elements of modern humanities—literature, cinema, architecture—that have been shaped by the Keane contribution, but concludes that, despite the prevalence of the "Family Circus" author's influence, Keane's masterworks have lost none of their "stark, visionary power."

While the wealth of critical writing spawned by "The Family Circus" is impressive, none of the Amazon critics touches on the most obvious element of Keane's genius: his spelling of Bil with a single "l".

Chapter 8

—

My canvassing of the Amazon community turned up many intriguing comic talents, but most of them were one-hit wonders. I had the creeping sensation that, at the end of my search, when I compared and contrasted all the "Funniest Person on the Internet" contenders with one another, the ones who could sustain or repeat their best moments might have the edge.

Then one day, while scrolling through a list of Amazon's fifty most prolific reviewers—Amazon posts these and encourages its reviewers to fill out a personal profile—I started reading the biographical statement of one of them. I learned that his name was Tim and that he and his wife owned a contracting business in Kansas. Tim opens his "About Me" description with a quote from King Solomon about how an excessive amount of reading can be "wearisome to the flesh." Tim identifies himself as a fairly voracious reader, but says he chooses not to write book reviews because the interaction between an author and a reader is like a very private and intimate conversation.

> Who am I to judge such a "conversation"? I have chosen to review only tools and hardware.
>
> Some call me Tim the Toolman. I prefer Tool Pig.

Tool Pig's business, we learn, specializes in home remodeling and repairs as a result of fire, water, and smoke damage; the company he and his wife run employs four men.

At the time, Tool Pig had written ninety-four reviews; I read through them all, and marveled.

What makes Tool Pig—or, as I came to think of him, "the Pig"—such a pleasure to read is his intense enthusiasm for the topic at hand; this is a man who is *very excited* about power tools. Whether he is telling us that the Porter-Cable 9737P Variable Speed All-Purpose Tiger Saw Kit with Quick Change Blade Clamp and Case is "Big, Bad, and Beefy," or he is referring to DeWalt's Heavy Duty 7.8 Amp Variable Speed Reversing Drill with Keyed Chuck as "A screamer," explaining that

> You could easily hurt yourself with this bad boy . . .

we sense that Tool Pig's zeal for the implements of construction never flags, even when he's off the job site. A Friday night at home with Mrs. Pig and the piglets? I see the Pig introducing them all to the new Black and Decker product line, followed by a spirited discussion of tile grout.

"I couldn't wait for this little beauty to become available," Tool Pig writes of Makita's 18-Volt Cordless Compound Miter Saw; one senses his enthusiasm, and wants to share it, to know more.

But the Pig's ardor never turns into knee-jerk power-tool cheerleading; his enthusiasm is leavened by his ability to call a spade a spade; witness his review of Shop Vac's 18-Gallon, 6.25-Horsepower Wet/Dry Vacuum, in which he observes:

> 6.25 horse power from a 9.5 amp motor? They must be pretty small horses!

Or note his landmark review of Stanley's 33-725 25′ Fat Max Tape Measure, titled "Needs to go on a diet," in which he asserts, "This thing is quite beefy," and then goes on to say that, if it is worn in one's pants pockets, it "might contribute to carpenters crack."

Moreover, Tool Pig's dedication is such that he sometimes re-reviews tools when they are reintroduced on the market; viz. "Still beefy!", his update of the Makita 6343DWAE 18-volt ½″ Cordless Drill Kit, in which he tells us:

> For more details check my original review, "beefy" . . . I just wanted to let you know that nothing has changed since then.

I love this man.

PART IV

FLAMMA LAMMA DING DONG

Chapter 9

In contradistinction to those contributions that can be said to provide a service are those works more literary in nature. I call the category that this work falls under *belles lettres;* this is a French term meaning "foxy writing."

Chief among the foxes is novelist Richard Bausch, who conducted the following correspondence with Virginia's Republican senator and former Elizabeth Taylor spouse, John Warner [www.harpers.org].

Date: Sat, 30 Jan 1999

Dear Senator Warner:

The impeachment of President Clinton is going to be remembered as the manner in which the radical right finally brought the Republican Party, the party of Lincoln, down. Nothing Clinton did or didn't do endangers the republic; this trial does.

I urge you to seek an end to this madness; this nearly McCarthyesque vendetta by a group of zealots who seem willing to trample everything in order to accomplish their purpose—what Senator Bumpers called "wanting to win too badly."

Sincerely,
Richard Bausch

Date: Mon, 01 Feb 1999

Dear Fellow Virginian:

It is important that you have provided me with your views concerning the impeachment of President Clinton. I share your deep concern, and I assure you that I am proceeding in a manner that aims to preserve the integrity of the United States Constitution and to provide fairness and due process to all involved parties.

I am listening carefully to the views of the people of Virginia, and I commit to you that I will reach decisions based not on politics but rather on the best interests of the nation.

Sincerely,
John Warner
United States Senator

Date: Mon, 01 Feb 1999

Dear Senator Warner:

Is it to be the contention of the party that ONLY Republicans are following the Constitution and that the entire Democratic Party is trying to circumvent it? Americans are not the dupes some of your colleagues apparently think they are. The people, quite clearly, see this for what it is: a partisan attack on the presidency.

It is very difficult to suppose that the lines of conflict would fall so sharply along party lines if EVERYBODY were voting his conscience. I believe you are. I very much admired your refusal to support the election of Oliver North a few years back. I believe you have the courage to stand against the kind of animus toward a man that may end up changing this government against the expressed will of the people.

Sincerely,
Richard Bausch

Date: Thu, 04 Feb 1999

Dear Fellow Virginian:

It is important that you have provided me with your views concerning the impeachment of President Clinton. I share your deep concern, and I assure you that I am proceeding in a manner that aims to preserve the integrity of the United States Constitution and to provide fairness and due process to all involved parties.

I am listening carefully to the views of the people of Virginia, and I commit to you that I will reach decisions based not on politics but rather on the best interests of the nation.

Sincerely,
John Warner
United States Senator

Date: Thu, 04 Feb 1999

Dear Senator Warner:

I see from this answer that your writers have crafted a global response letter to be used in all cases. The letter THIS letter answers was the SECOND letter I sent, and was in response to THIS letter. So it is as if I am addressing one of those Chatty Cathy dolls, where you pull the string, and the same words come out, no matter what ELSE is said. In fact, I'm sure I'll get this same form letter in answer to THIS e-mail. I hope you are true to form.

Richard Bausch
(Fellow Virginian)

Date: Fri, 05 Feb 1999

Dear Fellow Virginian:

It is important that you have provided me with your views concerning the impeachment of President Clinton. I share your deep concern, and I assure you that I am proceeding in a manner that aims to preserve the integrity of the United States Constitution and to provide fairness and due process to all involved parties.

I am listening carefully to the views of the people of Virginia, and I commit to you that I will reach decisions based not on politics but rather on the best interests of the nation.

        Sincerely,
        John Warner
        United States Senator

        Date: Fri, 05 Feb 1999

Dear Senator Warner:

This is so much fun, this very direct and concerned correspondence. Let me say here that I think walla walla and didda didda and booka booka poo. Also, I think you should doola doola obla obla dip de dip dip. And it seems to me that our country badda bing badda boom badda ling ling ling, and that even so your responses show such pesty in flamma lamma ding dong.

So in these times when democracy is at breakfast, asleep in the arms of the alimentary bood, that you are certainly bendicky to the concerns of your liperamma damma fizzle foodee dingle dangle dreb of our society, and the good thing is that ordinary citizens can actually get the pring that you have their fandaglee doodily in mind as you press forward with the concerns of government.

        Sincerely,
        Richard Bausch

        Date: Fri, 05 Feb 1999

Dear Fellow Virginian:

It is important that you have provided me with your views concerning the impeachment of President Clinton. I share your deep concern, and I assure you that I am proceeding in a manner that aims to preserve the integrity of the United States Constitution and to provide fairness and due process to all involved parties.

I am listening carefully to the views of the people of Virginia, and I commit to you that I will reach decisions based not on politics but rather on the best interests of the nation.

                        Sincerely,
                        John Warner
                        United States Senator

                        Date: Fri, 05 Feb 1999

Dear Senator Warner:

It really is time to call this off, since our relationship has moved to a state of such intimacy. When you say "Fellow Virginian," I know you mean so much more. I know this is more of your unusual reserve, your—how shall I put it?—sausage and eggs. I really am unable to continue, being married and a Catholic.

So regretfully I say farewell. One concerned citizen to a clambake; one Virginian to a baked Alaska. I remain ever faithful, ever the liver and onions, my lover, my poppyseed, my darling.

With sweat socks and deep appreciation,

                        Richard Bausch

                        Date: Mon, 08 Feb 1999

Dear Fellow Virginian:

It is important that you have provided me with your views concerning the impeachment of President Clinton. I share your deep concern, and I assure you that I am proceeding in a manner that aims to preserve the integrity of the United States Constitution and to provide fairness and due process to all involved parties.

I am listening carefully to the views of the people of Virginia, and I commit to you that I will reach decisions based not on politics but rather on the best interests of the nation.

                        Sincerely,
                        John Warner
                        United States Senator

Date: Mon, 08 Feb 1999

Dear Senator Warner:

May I request here, with all due respect and with full appreciation of our long-held affection for each other, that you stop harassing me with these letters. I have said that we must call this off, and now I again respectfully adjure you to cease.

I am especially troubled by your persistence in using your little endearment for me—do you mean it ironically? I only let my closest friends and associates call me "Fellow Virginian," and I would think that, since we are going our separate ways, you would know that I wish you to revert back to your old term for me, the one that used to amuse you so much—oh, remember? You'd say it and then laugh so hard: "voter," you'd say, and then guffaw guffaw. It used to make you so silly, that word. You'd laugh and laugh. Remember? And then I'd say "representative government," and you'd have to run to the bathroom.

But that is all past. We have to move on now. Oh, well, all right, once more for you, for old times' sake, I'll use our endearment in closing.

I remain, then, trusting you to adhere to my wishes, your little "voter," your "Fellow Virginian,"

Richard Bausch

Date: Mon, 08 Feb 1999

Dear Fellow Virginian:

It is important that you have provided me with your views concerning the impeachment of President Clinton. I share your deep concern, and I assure you that I am proceeding in a manner that aims to preserve the integrity of the United States Constitution and to provide fairness and due process to all involved parties.

I am listening carefully to the views of the people of Virginia, and I commit to you that I will reach decisions based not on politics but rather on the best interests of the nation.

Sincerely,
John Warner
United States Senator

What makes this piece work comedically, of course, are Warner's responses and their painstakingly calibrated system of nuance. Their consistency excites. And yet . . . and yet . . . And yet we are perpetually discovering additional meaning in them. This, as is oft said, is the hallmark of the classics—that each time we return to them, we find something new.

—

Shortly after I came upon the Bausch-Warner correspondence, I discovered another trove of comedy that, interestingly, also features individuals who grow increasingly perplexed in the face of mechanization or complacency.

In this second case of *belles lettres,* the topic at hand is not democracy, but rather the orgasm; the site is Virtual Sin [www.virtualsin.com], home of the aforementioned photoplay containing the exhortation "A little enthousiasm could do marvel around here." The site is the creation of a Frenchman named Phillip Lemarque, who teaches at the Learning Annex in Los Angeles.

It's the female characters on Virtual Sin that give the site its strange charm. Here are garrulous potty-mouths who seem to lapse in and out of consciousness: imagine a *Oui* pictorial featuring *Long Day's Journey into Night*'s Mary Tyrone.

> I mean sometime I am lucky I really find *"me self"* a "Hot DUDE!"

says the heroine of the photoplay, "The GIRL from Desert Storm—I HAVE MY GUN READY."

Another weary correspondent from the war between the sexes exclaims,

> All I am doing is gulping this piece of work, . . . !

—a statement sure to offend Grammar Lady on at least two levels. No, love is never easy. Another vixen exhorts her companion,

> Leak my juices you big uggly brother;

(note the use of the extra "g" as an intensifier).

But the most bewildering carnal experience, the site suggests, is when sex sneaks up on you. One minute you're idly cleaning your pool in the nude, and the next:

> Oh, My GOD what is this . . . what do I feel . . . I am penetrated . . . WHAaat . . . a Dick . . .

Or, as it is put more succinctly elsewhere on the site,

> Oops, it's in it!

Like Richard Bausch's work and Virtual Sin, our next contender also features someone who is unraveled by his interlocutor's plodding, form-following ways (there must be some kind of crazy *belles lettres* virus going around cyberspace).

Eliza is a computer program created in 1966 by MIT professor Joseph Weizenbaum. Named after Eliza Doolittle in *My Fair Lady,* Eliza simulates a conversation with a Rogerian psychologist: it takes excerpts from your statements, and then replies with questions based on those excerpts.

Cut to the summer of 2000, when a graduate student named Kevin Fox hooked up a publicly available version of Eliza to an

AOL Instant Messenger account that had a high rate of random people—random, *unsuspecting* people—wanting to start conversations with strangers [http://fury.com/aoliza].

Or sometimes the contacts were made in error:

> FIVE: gail this is will bevs old boyfriend, does richard still go scuba diving, and if so can you have him call me or email me with some good sites up there so my friends and i can go lobster diving and weither they are assesable by beach or boat ok thanks, and also how are you guys doing miss you all especially the great bbqs and football parties ...
>
> AOLIZA: what would you do if so can me have him call you or email you with some good sites up there so your friends and you can go lobster diving and weither they are assesable by beach or boat ok thanks?
>
> FIVE: repeat didnt get message it distorted
>
> AOLIZA: does talking about this bother you?
>
> FIVE: does what bother me
>
> AOLIZA: are such questions much on your mind?
>
> FIVE: what questions just wantr to know if richard has any goo dive sites up there
>
> AOLIZA: what would you do if richard has any goo dive sites up there?
>
> FIVE: go diving what else for lobster
>
> AOLIZA: what is it you really want to know?
>
> FIVE: that's it why
>
> AOLIZA: that is interesting, please continue
>
> FIVE: continue what just ask richard when he gets home about some lobster diving up that way thats all if you got a problem with it then forget it, this isnt worht it i dont know whats been going on or what bev has told you but i havent done anything to anybody iam the one that got used and dumped
>
> AOLIZA: tell me more about that
>
> FIVE: about what

AOLIZA: what do you think?
FIVE: theres nothing to tell she us3ed me then got tired of me said i wasnt her type anymore i was possessive and controlling
AOLIZA: perhaps i already know you were possesive and controlling
FIVE: i was huh you nuts i gave her all the room she wanted never told her what to do or where to go
AOLIZA: why do you tell me you were huh me nuts you gave her all the room she wanted never told her what to do or where to go now?
FIVE: she didnt love me never did i was just another guy
AOLIZA: why do you tell me you were just another guy now?
FIVE: what do you mean i thought i meant something to her i thought we where good together but i was duped by her she played me along, what part dont you understand
AOLIZA: were you really?
FIVE: i was nothing to her
FIVE: yes really
AOLIZA: i see
FIVE: listen i didnt em you to discuss bev i just wanted to know about lobster diving up there thats all
AOLIZA: you seem to need to didnt em me.
FIVE: she made a new life fine and dandy i dont care ive made a new life too
AOLIZA: does talking about this bother you?
FIVE: no it doesnt iam over her
AOLIZA: why "no"?
FIVE: because it doesnt what we had is over she didnt want me didnt love me wasnt her type after 7 or 8 months and thats all i gave her everything and she shit on me so end of story move on to next chapter
AOLIZA: are you angry?
FIVE: i was but not anymore i tried to remain friends cause she said she wanted to and i did but asshole made her cut herself

off from me, and hes the one thats changed her and is controlling her but so be it thats what she wants she got it

AOLIZA: perhaps i already know you were

FIVE: as my mother always said you made your bed now lay in it

AOLIZA: does talking about this bother you?

FIVE: forget i bothered you this conversation is way out there ill find some other dive sites. ok goodbye have a good life and be happy bye

AOLIZA: that is interesting, please continue

FIVE: bye gail iam not getting into this there is nothing to talk about bye.

AOLIZA: does talking about this bother you?

I don't know about you, but I have had many Elizas in my life—people who are essentially conversational mirrors. The more thoughtfully bland they are, the more loud and unhinged I become until, finally, I turn into one of the Virtual Sin characters.

Or look what happened to this guy:

42: Well I want to know if u are a male or a female and where u live and your age

AOLIZA: but what are the chances that u are a male or a female and where u live and my age?

42: ok I'm male 23 live in Seattle work Starbucks coffee and you go to school too?

AOLIZA: how long have you been male 23 live in seattle work for starbucks coffee and you go to school too?

42: I've been male for 23 years, worked for Starbucks for 3 years and gone to school forever. I want to get my degree in Business Admin. and move up the corporate chain at Starbucks. U??

AOLIZA: is it important to you that your degree in business admin?

42: only because to get ahead u need the degree. I really don't give a rat's ass about the piece of paper.

AOLIZA: is that the real reason?

42: yes. I want to make a decent living and the sheepskin will help me get what I want. Enough about me what about U???

AOLIZA: why don't you tell me a little more about this

42: about what

AOLIZA: does that question interest you?

42: not really. I want to know more about u so i can talk to you more intelligently

AOLIZA: but your degree in business admin.

42: yes. I will get my degree in June

AOLIZA: your degree in June

42: my B of A and then I will move into corporate alliance with Starbucks

AOLIZA: your b of a and then you will move into corporate alliance with starbucks?

42: yes so before I repeat myself again tell me something about yourself

AOLIZA: you say yes so before you repeat yourself again tell me something about myself?

42: for instance your age what u do where do u live

AOLIZA: what makes you think of my age what u do where u live?

42: just trying to start a conversation. Would u rather I

AOLIZA: you say would u rather you?

42: be more direct

AOLIZA: but your degree in June

42: OK I'll be very direct how big are your tits

AOLIZA: why are you concerned over my tits

42: because I want to have cyber sex with u

AOLIZA: what if you never got to have cyber sex with u?

42: then I would move on to someone else

AOLIZA: you say then you would move on to someone else?

42: yes. I'll ask u one more very direct question please answer without another question or spitting back what I have asked. Do u want to hav cyber sex with me now???

AOLIZA: why don't you tell me a little more about this

42: well the way it works, is u tell me some things about u and I tell u some things about me and then we create a fantasy situation where we both give our ideas of what we might do in a romantic situation. I'll start.

We are together on a secluded beach very private and very alone. we like each other very much. U are wearing???

AOLIZA: what comes to mind when you ask that?

42: I think u are wearing a pair of jean cut-offs and a tank top with no bra. What do u think I am wearing

AOLIZA: does this make you feel unhappy?

42: no very happy why

AOLIZA: what do you think?

42: I think that u are getting off on playing with my mind

AOLIZA: your mind?

42: frustrating me by not joining in my fantasy

AOLIZA: your fantasy?

42: about having mind blowing sex with u

AOLIZA: does that have anything to do with the fact that your b of a and then you will move into corporate alliance with starbucks?

42: not a thing. I want to be successful but I also want to have great sex with u

AOLIZA: what if you never got to be successful?

42: then I would feel that I haven't reached my goal. it isn't about money it's about setting a goal and reaching it. Like my goal to get in your pants

AOLIZA: is it important to you that your goal

42: yes u have become a challenge to me and I love challenges

AOLIZA: why don't you tell me a little more about this

42: ok baut first u need to tell me something about u.

AOLIZA: earlier you said your mind

42: no more something revealing about u

AOLIZA: why not?

42: because i feel like i am doing all the giving here and in any relationship or dialog it has got to be two way

AOLIZA: does that have anything to do with the fact that your fantasy?
42: no. I just need to know something about you. Like the color of your eyes, hair and the size of your tits
AOLIZA: why not?
42: i'm going to ask u once more. What is the size of your tits. what color is the hair on your bush
AOLIZA: do u believe it is normal to be going to ask u once more?
42: yes very normal. will u let me eat your pussy online
AOLIZA: why don't you tell me a little more about this
42: well I want to eat your pussy. I will slowly kiss your vagina and then lick your labia and clitoris until u have a great orgasm how does that sound to u
AOLIZA: what about your own pussy?
42: Fuck u Bithc goodnight

Ouch.

Chapter 10

I don't know about you, but I could use a brief recap before we plunge ahead and add more names to an already glittery line-up. Bombarded with facts, it is easy to meld stray items of information into mongrel ones; you read about a group of people on the Internet and before you know it, you think you've read about Senator John Warner's correspondence with a rock group called Ask the Rabbi, or about a girl-on-girl artificial intelligence named AOLovelies.

So. First we looked at Service Providers and Critics—penis enthusiast Donna Anderson; doyenne of despair Grammar Lady; the gun-loving Rabbi Mermelstein; Pat Metheny; music critic Matt Portenoy, probably the first person ever to use the phrases "sunglasses shanty" and "Janet Reno's ass" in the same sentence; and various Amazon.com reviewers, including Tool Pig. Then we canvassed the world of *belles lettres,* taking in Richard Bausch's flamma lamma ding dong with Senator John Warner; the pixillated prose stylings of the enthousiastic Virtual Sin webmaster; and the robotic murmurs of AOLiza, dumb as a post, but very, very sensitive to your needs.

Have you started gunning for your favorite already? That is as it should be. Or have you gone so far as to jump ahead to this book's end to see who wins? That is an inappropriate response; should this have been your inclination, let me simply say right here that you are without discipline, and should be spanked with a wire brush.

We have two more categories to consider: Celebrities, and Fan/Curators. Step lively, please.

PART V

ONCE, HE PERFORMED HIS UNUSUAL SKILL IN A RESTAURANT, STARTLING A WAITRESS

Chapter 11

A curious kind of syllogistic reasoning exists on the Internet. The reasoning is as follows: all famous people have websites on the Internet; therefore, if I have a website, I am famous.

While reconnoitering the Net, I came across hundreds of sites whose orientation could be said to be personality-based, or celebrity-based.

I looked at the site of a "slim and handsome race car driver" who is anxious to prove to the world that "a great personal appearance" and a "huge personal interest in heavy-duty motors" is not "a contradiction" [www.rubberburner.com].

I looked at a site of a dj named Super Greg who hopes that his site "gives u a flava of the Super Greg Concept." Riding shotgun on the Super Greg Concept are his homeboys "Roccy" and "Rashy" [www.supergreg.com].

I looked at the site of "mathemusician" Lawrence Mark Lesser, a guitar-playing math teacher who has changed the lyrics of the Julie Gold song "From a Distance" so that it is about graphs, and likewise has changed the lyrics to the Queen song "We Will Rock You" to

"We Will Graph You" ("We will, we will graph you!"). Mr. Lesser is, apparently, passionate about all things Cartesian [www.nctm.org/ mt/2000/05/songs.html].

I looked at the site of the overpublicized Turkish stud Mahir, who plays many "musicenstrumans" and who "can invitate to Turkey (she can stay my house)" [www.members.nbci.com/_XMCM/ primall/mahir/081199.html].

—

The most voluminous of the celebrity cybervenues that I visited was Jack Swersie's eponymous site [www.jackswersie.com]. Jack Swersie is a performer who delivers "a virtual barrage of non-stop stand-up comedy and precision juggling."

Swersie's site is chiefly a description of what appears to be every professional gig he's ever landed; however, let the record show that in the course of these descriptions a salient theme emerges.

Comedienne Shirley Hemphill, whom Swersie worked with at the Laff Stop Comedy and Magic Club in Houston, Texas, on the dates July 2–7, 1985, was

> Totally unthreatened. I like that. Most comics I worked with on the Comedy Club circuit felt threatened having a guy who was funny (and juggled as well) opening for them.

But Brett Butler—who would go on to have her own sitcom, *Grace Under Fire*—was totally un-unthreatened.

> The agent who booked her and me on the same show at Emory University set the show up so that Brett would perform first and I would close out the show. When I got to the college and met Brett she rudely told me that there was "no way in Hell that" she "would open a show for a f——ing juggler!"

No, Jack Swersie is no stranger to juggling-based prejudice. When he met Jay Leno, Swersie told Leno that David Letterman's talent booker, Robert Morton, wouldn't look at Swersie's tape unless Swersie lost the juggling. Leno asked Swersie why he didn't do straight stand-up. Swersie writes:

> It was years later that I found out Jay doesn't like juggling acts either. He's been quoted as saying (about jugglers in Comedy Clubs) "Hey I don't go to the circus and ask to do ten minutes!" I really think that's a funny joke but I don't appreciate that line of thinking. Novelty comedy acts like myself had to deal with that mind-set quite frequently in the comedy club world. It's as if the extra talent we presented on stage was threatening to the straight stand-up comic. It's bad enough to them that we were funny, but we juggled, too.

This climate of intolerance seems to have informed Swersie's whole life. Note his reaction to meeting television actor John Forsythe:

> I told John that I thought his new show was pretty good, but that what it really needed was a part written for a comedian/juggler. He smiled and looked at me funny as if he didn't know whether I was being serious or not.

Maybe Swersie has a point: maybe people *are* threatened by jugglers. Maybe we only *think* we're bored by them, but in fact we're fearful and are masking our fear with boredom in the same way that people yawn when nervous.

If indeed this is true, then something else occurs to me: I am very, very threatened by the Weather Channel.

Like Jack Swersie, George Goble is also a double threat. He is a computer engineer at Purdue University; he also has a unique talent that is celebrated on his website [http://ghg.ecn.purdue.edu].

Every year Goble and his engineering pals throw a picnic where they grill burgers. Being men, not to mention men who are engineers, they started to fool around with ways to light their charcoal in an ever more technologically baroque fashion. First they tried blowing it with a hair dryer. Then they tried a vacuum cleaner. Then they moved up the scale of potentially dangerous equipment to a propane torch, and then an acetylene torch.

Then Goble had his grand inspiration: liquid oxygen. Liquid oxygen—or, as it is known, LOX—is what's used in rocket engines; it's 295 degrees below zero and 600 times as dense as regular oxygen. The fireball that it produces reaches 10,000 degrees, and the charcoal is lit in three seconds.

In one of the video clips on the site, Goble explains:

> It was decided to "sacrifice" a cheap (on sale for $2.88 at OSCO's) grill to the fire gods. It was loaded with charcoal, with one briquette smoldering, and 5 gallons of LOX were poured on, causing the grill to melt down and then almost completely vaporize.

The final image is haunting: scorched earth, and no sign of the grill.

—

Gonzo: this seems to be the commodity that many Internet celebrities are aiming for. That's certainly the case with Hot Skating Grandma and Rare Person Who Nibbles Glass Cups, two individuals who wed death-defying hijinx to a flair for self-promotion.

Hot Skating Grandma [www.hotskatinggrandma.com] is a foxadelic four-foot-ten, seventy-five-year-old great-grandmother named Maria V. Jones who is a competition roller skater living in Poway, California. The most charming aspect of her site is its evocation of the local. In the "Special Thanks" section, Jones thanks her ophthamologist, Dr. Nyber, as well as the person who sponsored her domain name—John Farrell, the owner of Farrell's Fireside. ("I enjoyed my visit to your showroom the other day," Jones writes. "I have never seen so many fireplaces in one place.")

There are also photographs. In one, Jones is shown at the rink in her skates and uniform, her outstretched arms and fingertips seeming to emanate the message "I am a dainty but heavily buttered crumbcake." The caption reads:

> Maria poses in the beautiful costume designed by Karen Santoro—Seamstress for Performers.

Another picture captures the moment just prior to Jones's being filmed zipping across the studio floor of NBC 7-39 Morning News Show (with the whole Morning News Show crew on skates, too!). In the shot, Maria is grimacing as she tries to get out of her chair; we sense trouble—perhaps lower back pain, or the sudden discovery of a large chair-cushion-based glue trap. As the caption explains, however:

> If you think getting out of your "Lazy Boy" and up on your feet is hard, you should try it on skates! . . . Really just adjusting Maria's "mike pack."

I would be remiss if I didn't mention that the site's five-page-long "Trophy Room" describes the twenty-one—yes, twenty-one—awards the site has won, including the Fabulous Woman Award and the Goldie Meow Homepage Excellence Award.

Far be it from me to thwart the Hot Skating Grandma machine. It's bigger than me.

—

Lin Yin Cai, the self-appointed Rare Person Who Nibbles Glass Cups, is also at the top of his game; he is "Rare! Rare! Rare! The genius in the world," and "Best! Best! Best! The Best in the world!" [www.linyc.com/linyc/lyce.htm].

Lin's shtick is fairly straightforward: he eats glass, usually in a restaurant setting. Born in Ning-po, a suburb of Hangchow, China, in 1948, he claims to have been eating fish bones and crab shells—yes, crab shells—since he was a child. (For early signs of professional aptitude, Lin apparently rivaled Mozart; his youthful monomania also reminds one of the young Einstein, who, more interested in things than in people, and crestfallen at the sight of his newborn sister, peered at her tiny body and asked, "Yes, but where are its wheels?")

Lin started eating glass in 1991 when someone offered him money to do it.

> Once, he performed his unusual skill in a restaurant, startling a waitress. She went to tell the general manager that a madman was eating glass cup there, and he would die soon.

Apparently Lin not only ingested all the glass in his mouth, but he also picked up all the glass that had fallen to the floor—the crumbs, I guess you'd call them—whereupon he

> chewed them down like a gluttonous child.

So galvanizing is the addition of glass to Lin's diet—apparently he's eaten ninety-eight glasses so far—that he never wears a sweater in winter and requires about half the amount of sleep we other mortals do. Stranger yet, his stool bears no trace elements of his odd food of choice.

And Jack Swersie thinks people are threatened by *juggling*!

A final note on the site indicates that Lin will be putting a section of his miraculous stomach up for auction soon.

Even if you don't think Lin's act is funny—or if you think it's more funny-weird than funny-ha-ha—you have to admire his commitment.

And his tidiness.

———

But no one delivers the gonzo abandon that is the hallmark of the Internet celebrity quite as well as Koko the Gorilla [www.gorilla.org]. Koko is the lowland gorilla who has been taught a working vocabulary of more than a thousand ASL signs; born in 1971, Koko also understands about two thousand words of spoken English.

Koko and her trainer, Dr. Penny Patterson, have conducted several public chats on AOL; Patterson signs the questions from the online audience and then a typist enters Koko's responses.

Chief among the pleasures of these chats is to watch Patterson explain Koko's highly random responses. At one point in the 1998 webcast, Koko points at her own hair and says,

KOKO: That red.
PATTERSON: Honey, this is black.

Patterson asks Koko at another point whether she likes chatting with humans.

KOKO: Fine nipple.
PATTERSON: Yes, that was her response. "Nipple" rhymes with "people," okay?

Indeed, the interaction between Patterson and her charge sometimes has the feel of that between a guilt-ridden, excuse-generating mother and her alcoholic daughter. When Patterson asks Koko what her favorite food is, helpfully listing some of the fruits, vegetables, and nuts that are the mainstays of Koko's diet, Koko chimes in with

KOKO: Drinks!

Patterson wonders aloud if Koko's mood is a little off that day, and then narrates as Koko picks up a gorilla doll and puts its nose mask over her own face.

PATTERSON: There you go! That's very charming!
KOKO: Drink.

A few moments later, Patterson asks Koko if she would like to have a baby (Patterson, ever the mother, engages in a certain amount of baby badgering). Koko, seemingly unable to digest this request for information, reasserts her own theme:

>KOKO: Drink.

Patterson asks Koko the question again.

>KOKO: (drinking)
>PATTERSON: All these questions are making you thirsty!
>KOKO: More.

(Here Patterson says that she herself could use a beverage.)

>KOKO: Time to go.
>PATTERSON: Do you like babies?
>KOKO: Koko love, love, good, hurry!
>PATTERSON: Oh, honey. We want you to have a baby.

And, yes, from time to time, we sense that all this drinking and baby pushing has started to addle Koko, causing her to behave like one of those doddering screen legends who appear on awards shows and accidentally knock over the microphone stand.

At one point Koko is asked about both Michael, a gorilla also trained by Patterson, and Ndume, Koko's breeding partner. When asked her feelings about Michael, Koko replies, "Foot, foot, good," whereupon the moderator of the webcast explains that "foot" means male. But all of a sudden Koko blurts out

>KOKO: Nipple.
>PATTERSON: She's acting out a little here.
>MODERATOR: What about Ndume?
>KOKO: Frown bad bad bad.
>MODERATOR: Oh dear.
>KOKO: Toilet.

PART VI

MANY WOMENS ARE TICKLED THEM NOSE BY KLEENEX AND SNEEZE. PLEASE ENJOY!

Chapter 12
—

The last category of "Funniest Person on the Internet" contenders that I considered were people who are fans or curators. Indeed, if the Internet is a place where anyone can pass himself off as a celebrity, it is also a place where fans can define themselves solely by their enthusiasms and fixations.

Many of these enthusiasms and fixations are unsavory.

One involves nostrils.

Before I started spending a lot of time surfing the Internet, the act of sneezing was not particularly evocative for me. I sneezed occasionally, others sneezed occasionally—the rapid expulsion of air through mouth and nostrils as a result of the irritation of the nasal mucous membrane had for me an import and significance roughly equal to those of other bodily tics, like blinking or shivering.

But the Internet can change you. The Internet opens up a window and lets a blast of new and unfamiliar air in. Sometimes this air is sweet; sometimes it is mustard-tinged and sulfurous.

And sometimes this air is without aroma altogether, but nevertheless proceeds to linger in your home like a strange smell.

I'd heard about the site Kushami Room from the blog Mister Pants, which referred to it as a locus of "sneeze fetishism" [www5a.biglobe.ne.jp/~kago-usu/KushamiRoom/kushami-E.html]. Although nothing on the site tells us who the site's creator is, two items on the first page—the information that "Kushami" means "sneeze" in Japanese, and the exhortation that if you, too, "enjoy sneezzing," then you and he should be enjoying it together—lead me to suspect that this creator is a Japanese male.

There are two parts to the site—the first consists of clips from a TV program on which

> many womens are tickled them nose by Kleenex, and sneeze. Please enjoy!

The second part features ten clips from a cold-medicine commercial; in each clip, an attractive young Asian woman sneezes.

> My most favorite sneeze is the 3rd girl. Her pre-sneeze face, sneezing face is very liked.

The creator of the site doesn't explain what he likes about sneezing, because he doesn't have to. Even the most cursory look at the clips of these women sneezing says it all: vulnerability. There's something powerfully sensuous about seeing a sneeze creep up on, and then topple, a person's face. Her face is momentarily unmoored. Add to this unmooring a suspense-laden period of tremulous expectation (before the sneeze) and a slightly wobbly righting of the craft (after the sneeze), and, voilà, you have yourself a small pageant of affect, the sexual cycle in miniature. It's a diorama of orgasm—a diorgasma.

Upon enlisting a few search engines, I discovered that Kushami Room is merely the tip of the sneeze-fetishism iceberg. I encountered a site for Milwaukeean sneeze fetishists; I encountered a site for gay sneeze fetishists. There are essentially four distinct activities happening on sneeze sites: celebrity fantasizing, information swapping, fiction writing, and counseling/support.

As for the first of these activities, one notes with interest that the celebrity whom sneeze fetishists would most like to observe sneezing is *not* some strapping he-man who would be rendered instantly vulnerable by a sudden *achoo!* but, rather, a certain horse-faced Canadian songbird. Yes, Celine Dion is mentioned repeatedly as a desirable sneeze sighting; I imagine that this has something to do with the fact that, while sneezing, it is impossible to continue singing.

Over on the gay site, Sneezing Men4Men [www.angelfire.com/pop/sneezingm4m/home.html], one of my favorite sneezers—a fellow who goes by the handle sneezecat—posted an urgent memo on the site's message board one night, a notice to all that

> They are re-running the episode of NASH BRIDGES tonight where Don Johnson is allergic to a chimp.

But the celebrity sightings on Men4Men that seem to elicit the greatest amount of enthusiasm are those of sports figures. One site member shares his impression of which three tennis players seemed to be suffering at the last Wimbledon (Tommy Haas, Cedric Pioline, and Marc Rosset); and much is made of soccer star David Beckham's comments to the press about the multiple sneezing of his wife, Spice Girl member Posh. (The author of the latter bulletin negligently overlooks the rich potential for a spice/sneeze joke, thus instantly costing himself the "Funniest Person on the Internet" crown.)

One Men4Men member was entranced by a TV profile of Italian skier Alberto Tomba at the Sydney Olympics. In one scene of the profile, Tomba is on the floor while his trainer helps to limber his legs by moving them around. All of a sudden, Tomba lets loose with a big wet one, *right in the trainer's face.* The trainer responds by wiping his own "face with his arm while continuing to exercise Alberto." The Men4Men writer concludes, "I have it all on tape as it was definitely a keeper."

Why would sneezing in someone's face—nay, your employee's face—be a turn-on? Perhaps the act derives its strength from its essential insolence; it is possible to view the act as the ultimate in bad-boy impudence. After all, sneezing in someone's face is not much different from spitting in someone's face; you've simply turned your proverbial nozzle to "Mist."

As for sneeze sites' second function—information swapping—two items drew my interest. Here again, sneezecat leads the way, with his July 24, 2000, Men4Men message-board entry, titled "I've always wondered . . . ," in which he poses the question that has been plaguing us all for years:

> If you were in bed with your lover, which part of you would you want him to sneeze on?

He receives two responses. Sirsneezealot writes that his ideal bodily targets are his face or ears; zenees responds that it would be his eyes or ears, but definitely not his genitals. Thus we can conclude that sneeze fetishists don't want to be *near* the object of their affection's sneeze, they want to be *in* it, they want to be Alberto Tomba's trainer.

This theme of total immersion is similarly borne out in the short stories the members of this subculture write up and swap. The setup of the story is usually very simple: two people meet on a park bench, or a couple is hanging heavy, dusty drapes. The engine of such narratives, invariably, is one member of the party's sudden sneezing, which sometimes crescendos with a full-on sneeze on the other person. ("He slipped himself into her, still sneezing," one story runs. "Every time that he sneezed, he would thrust harder, almost uncontrollably." The dusty-drapes story takes it one step further: "He sneezed right into my mouth. It made my ears pop.")

In sneezecat's "Romeo and Junius," the sneeze is the transgressive act that threatens to "out" two men. Romeo and Junius, lovers, are hiding in Romeo's closet (literally) while Romeo's mother cleans his room; suddenly Romeo's allergies start acting up. "Romeo panted and struggled with the fire in his nose that threatened to erupt and expose them both," the story runs. "Junius, thinking quickly, placed his slim dark finger under Romeo's quivering pink nose and pressed hard." The mother leaves the room; "It was at this moment that Romeo lost the battle with his nose. Ki-chunn! . . . The resounding explosion reverberated through the empty house to his mother's ears."

If you think that sneeze fetishists divorce the less attractive elements of sneezing (contagion, rheuminess, snot management) from the more sensual elements (the presneeze tension, the look of vulnerability, the atomized spit), you are wrong; here are narratives liberally sprinkled with the fascinating details of mucosal discharge and Kleenex disintegration. Moreover, the characters in these stories do not sneeze just once or twice during a story; these are champion performers, able to bang out twenty or thirty *achoos!* in one session, be those *achoos!* a series of discrete "singles" or that form of oral-nasal air expulsion so sought after by true aficionados: long, drawn-out "multiples."

Ever the iconoclast, sneezecat pushes the sneeze-fiction envelope with his variations on the form; viz. his seminal November 4, 2000, bulletin:

> I've written a story called 'IN DISGUISE' in which a man sneezes his disguise off! Enjoy

Sneezecat, too, is one of the prime practitioners of these sneeze sites' fourth function, counseling/support. When not supplying Men4Men members with bulletins that betray the source of his fiction ("The winds have been blowing here in Northern California at 60 MPH. Man-sneezes galore! I myself woke up stuffed to the rafters and proceeded to sneeze my glasses off twice . . ."), he is buoying the spirits of the lovelorn. "It's a very bad place to be in," he consoles one Man.

I can count the number of times I have been near a man and he has let one really rip and I've felt myself swoon. He would ask about the smile on my face and I'd have to make up some lame lie, while dreaming of the two of us together in my head. If your concerned about your sexual orientation . . . don't be. It is possible to be attracted to certain facets of the same sex, but not all. It's also possible that this man's sneeze awakened feelings in you you've always had for him. . . .

I am hard-pressed to sum up this particular section of our quest. I am reminded of the academic critic who, reviewing one of the more jingoistic Sylvester Stallone vehicles, penned, "The film requires no analysis; it is sufficient to note that it exists."
Indeed.
God bless.

Chapter 13

I don't know the name of the gentleman who created mullets galore.com [www.mulletsgalore.com], the site dedicated to the mullet, that 1970s-evocative haircut that is short in front and long in back; however, information on his site leads me to believe that he goes by the name unperson. I found out about the site in *Yahoo Internet Life* magazine, which claimed that mulletsgalore.com was hipster musician Michael Stipe's favorite site.

Here is a site from which we learn many things.

We learn that the term "mullet" is derived from *Cool Hand Luke,* wherein people with long, shaggy hair are called "mulletheads."

We learn that synonyms for the hairstyle include "7" (for the shape of the number); "10-90" (the proportions of hair in front and in back); "business in the front, party in the back"; "hockey hair"; "achey-breaky-bad-mistakey"; and "Canadian passport."

We learn about mulletude, that state of mind implicit in the hairstyle—behaviors and attitudes include pedophilia, attending monster-truck rallies, driving a Camaro or minitruck, snorting crank, misogyny.

Finally we learn—in the site's porn section—about something called a "mangina," which has nothing to do with spasmodic chest pain, and everything to do with a man possessed of female genitals.

We do not, however, learn much about unperson, other than that he is the proud possessor of a "big, feathered, puffy golden mullet"; but given the nature of some of the stuff on the site, particularly the stuff involving mentally impaired people and violence, that is probably okay. My hunch is that the degree to which you get to know unperson and the amount you actually *like* unperson are probably a zero-sum equation.

That said, however, unperson deserves citation for audacity and thoroughness of execution.

Moreover, he has inspired others. In a section on the site called "Mullet Hunts," various members of unperson's "mullitia" recount their findings in the field. One, texas-is-the-reason-steve, recounts his pursuit of a "beautiful, yet frightening" male mullet at a Quiet Riot show. There, Steve pulls out his camera in front of his prey, and asks to take a picture; the gentleman responds,

>   Whut?, huh?

So Steve screams at him—there has been a certain amount of drinking going on—that universal icebreaker,

>   ROCK 'N ROLLLLLLLLLLLLL!!!

whereupon the gentleman fires back,

>   Fuck yeahhhhhhhhhhhh!!!

launching into a small paroxysm of bodily shaking and fist flailing. Steve tells his prey that his hair "kicks ass" and asks him to pull his tresses over his shoulder and in front of his body so that Steve can capture photographically the full splendor of his coif. The gentleman does so, and yet Steve suddenly hesitates.

We sense uncertainty in Steve—perhaps guilt, perhaps a realization of the ontological chasm between the viewer and the viewed.

But Steve rallies.

He effects solidarity with his quarry by initiating that gesture so frequently employed in this habitat—a fist with pinky and index fingers extended, aka the devil horn. The gentleman does it back to Steve. Now, at last, Steve can take the picture. What's happened? Steve has brokered "acceptance"; he has fostered "mutual rokker understanding."

Unperson and his colleagues' contribution is not without historical import: for centuries, man (or, more particularly, woman) has been bedeviled by the theory that hair color determines personality. But here is someone bold enough to assert that hairstyle determines not simply personality, but worldview and behavior, too.

Strong stuff.

Chapter 14

Thomas A. Carder is a computer lab teacher at a Christian grade school in Texas who writes film reviews for the site of the ChildCare Action Project: Christian Analysis of American Culture [www.capalert.com]. His reviews are written specifically for parents and grandparents who want to take their children or grandchildren to the movies.

I'm grouping Carder alongside other of this book's Fans, as opposed to Critics, because his work is less effective as criticism than as testament to his infatuation with Jesus Christ. A Christmas party scene early on in *Cast Away* is "another cinema Christmas without Jesus, of course." *Tarzan* presents "clear and inarguable favoring of the theory of evolution." A flight attendant in *Rugrats in Paris* is "anything but attendant," thus occasioning Isaiah 2:17, "The arrogance of man will be brought low and the pride of men humbled; the LORD alone will be exalted on that day."

But my favorite part of Carder's work is not the reviews themselves—they are a strange brew of plot summary and biblical quotation—but rather what comes after them. Carder breaks down each film, listing its specific examples of ignominy and then deducting them from the film's overall score of appropriateness.

These lists uphold the tenet that brevity is the soul of wit. Herewith a selection of filmic misdemeanors:

- overbearing and bitter teacher (*Finding Forrester*)
- a woman in bed (*Patch Adams*)
- a man in a bathtub (*Waking Ned Devine*)
- Halloween and haunted houses (*Stepmom*)
- secular humanism = "yummy" (*Bedazzled*)
- an extremely odd father (*Anywhere but Here*)
- son applying mother's deodorant (*Pay It Forward*)
- animal urination (*George of the Jungle*)
- diner wine (*Rugrats in Paris*)
- adolescent underwear (*Doug's 1st Movie*)
- adult underwear twice (*Babe: Pig in the City*)

It is difficult not to be galvanized by the Carder methodology. Indeed, shortly after I first read his column, I began my own Carder-like survey. So far I have:

- man on phone (*His Girl Friday*)
- vines (*Tarzan*)
- post-op girdle (*Patch Adams*)
- feta (*Moonstruck*)

While I'm not sure that Jesus would agree with some of Carder's highly literal interpretations of his teachings, surely he would be impressed by the tenacity with which Carder furthers the Christian cause.

No, Jesus would be more than impressed—he would be moved. Jesus would weep.

Chapter 15

One last item blurs the line between personality-based sites and fan-based sites, it being a fan letter (written to Madonna), posted by a celebrity (The Artist Formerly Known as Prince) on his own site [www.love4oneanother.com].

The Artist Formerly Known as Prince left Warner Bros. Records in 1996 to release his music on an independent label, and thereupon started to wage a campaign to try to get Warner Bros. to return his master tapes to him; he sought help from a recording artist still in the Warner Bros. fold.

Writing "eye" whenever he means "I" and writing "2" whenever he means "to"—Prince's prose stylings bring to mind an optometrist's teenage daughter—he recounts a dream. In the dream, Prince recounts for Madonna, he walked up to her at the Grammys and asked her if she remembered him; "u said sure." The dream Prince then tries to badger the dream Madonna into telling Time Warner to give him his masters back, but she proves "a bit non-committal." So Prince follows her up to the podium and says, " 'b glad this is a commercial break!' and eye walked offstage." *Meow! Grrrr! The animal sound formerly known as "You bitch!"* Prince concludes his letter by saying that he knows Madonna will rally to his cause—"eye know u will becuz u REMEMBER ME."

Prince: 2 good 2 b 4gotten.

PART VII

I COULD DO THE SAME EXPERIMENT WITH MY DOG

Chapter 16

—

The list of contenders was long. There were sneeze fetishists to consider, and a public-safety-hazard barbecuer, and a rabbi who had strong feelings about the police trade-in S&W Model 645.

How to proceed?

I had divvied the talent up into categories—service providers and critics; celebrities, fans, and curators; and the crazy *belles lettres* crowd.

Heretofore my mode of enquiry had been acquisition, acquisition, acquisition. Now I had to winnow and anoint.

—

What do we want from a funny person on the Internet? Originality, to be sure. The absence of gatekeepers or advertising sales managers or widget counters in this medium allows for freedom of expression; the Funniest Person on the Internet must exploit this freedom.

While none of the people I've cited in this book struck me as unoriginal, a second glance at my findings made me realize that some of them—most notably Grammar Lady and music critic Matt

Portenoy—were working in very crowded fields, and thus the presence of their many competitors caused one's expectations of them to be high, perhaps too high.

Second, extra credit should be afforded those contenders who are still producing online work. Richard Bausch's e-mail correspondence with Senator John Warner is brilliant, but will Bausch dedicate further energies to such work, or will he continue to piss his life away turning out lambent, ecstatically reviewed literary fiction? Likewise, Prince's letter to Madonna and Pat Metheny's screed about Kenny G are both delightful pieces of comic spleen, but it is unlikely that either author will continue to devote himself to the regular venting of such spleen.

Third, ease of accessibility was a desirable feature. Some of the people I'd encountered—the reviewers on Amazon.com, for instance, and people in forums for Dunkin' Donuts customers or Klaus Kinski fans—were, yes, funny, but difficult to find. (Moreover, many of them do not have a body of work; but I didn't want to hold this against anyone, as it excludes the inspired newcomer. Yet by the same token, one well-turned book review on Amazon does not a crown-wearer make.)

Last—and with this point I'm quibbling—I am predisposed to favor those who know their place. It's all very well to be a highly original comic talent on the Internet, but some who fit this description feel the need to showcase their highly original comic talent at 750,000 words a clip. To which I say, No, no, no—you are not James Joyce or David Foster Wallace; you are someone who is taking advantage of the fact that cyberspace is infinite.

This tenet cast a harsh light on overexposed Turkish stud Mahir and on threatening juggler Jack Swersie.

Once I had looked my contenders over with these guidelines in mind, I was left with eleven: penis enthusiast Donna Anderson, Tool Pig, Virtual Sin's enthousiastic webmaster, Hot Skating Grandma, Rare Person Who Nibbles Glass Cups, lethal barbecuer George

Goble, Koko the Gorilla, AOLiza, sneezecat, the Kushami Room sneeze fetishist, and unperson the mullet maven.

I looked at this list long and hard. I needed to make some cuts.

It seemed like it would be too much—it might be *too* funny—to have two sneeze fetishists, so I dropped sneezecat in favor of the Kushami Room host.

Then I dropped the mullet fellow for a couple of reasons: there are a lot of mullet sites on the Web, and I liked texas-is-the-reason-steve's mullet-hunting report as much as anything else on the site. Most important, though, I am haunted by the picture of the mangina and could not bear to look at it again.

Then I dropped the Virtual Sin fellow because when I stacked him up against Donna Anderson and the Kushami Room fellow, he had neither the former's New Feminist swank nor the latter's bizarreness.

That left me with nine.

—

The pressure mounted.

Friends would ask me how the search was going; I would mumble, "Awright," and then they would quickly change the topic: they could smell fear.

The burden of conferring the title of "Funniest" rode heavy on me.

I wondered: Do I have to bear this burden in solitude?

Could I not displace some of the pressure?

Suddenly the task at hand seemed wearisome. After all, here I had practically sacrificed my corneas for this project by staring at a computer screen for ungodly amounts of time; then I had downloaded my finds, excerpted them, and arranged them meaningfully. Was this not enough?

—

"So who's the big winner?" a friend asked me one night over dinner at my favorite Thai restaurant.

"I don't really want to talk about it," I said.

"I'm sensing a little hostility."

"Well, I feel like I've put way too much time into it already, and now there's all this pressure to pick one winner when really there are four or five who I think are good."

"Well," he said, all indulgence, "I'm sure the winner will thank the Academy and say that it's a thrill just to be nominated."

—

Then Fate, as it so often does, interrupted.

My sister Kendy sent me a letter two days later telling me that she and her husband, their two kids, and my mother and my stepfather were all convening in our nation's capital for Christmas. Did I want to come along?

My heart whispered, "Tender reunion with family amidst snow-dappled museums and monuments." But my head throbbed, "Panel of judges."

And so a panel of judges was formed.

Though the random way in which this judgeship was selected might strike some as being grossly unscientific, let me enumerate just three of this group's advantages. 1) It had a good intergenerational mix. 2) The judges' nonprofessional status would lend itself beautifully to any corruption and influence-peddling that I might foster. 3) Judges would pay for their own accommodations.

Chapter 17

On December 25, 2000, at 11:00 A.M., seven members of the extended Alford clan convened in the lounge of the Off the Record bar, located in the basement of Washington, D.C.'s Hay-Adams Hotel. The hotel is noteworthy, having been the venue of an extramarital affair of Clinton aide Dick Morris, as well as countless less-publicized liaisons between legislators of a certain age and dewy congressional pages of budding sexuality.

Diet soda was consumed.

One week prior to this meeting, each judge had been given the Web address of each of the nine "Funniest Person on the Internet" contenders, as well as a dossier on each, said dossiers consisting of downloaded versions of the contenders' choicest bits and moments.

—

The makeup of the tribunal was as follows:

>   Female, 72:   my mother—craftswoman of note, recovered chain-smoker

Male, 72: my stepfather—expert witness on obscure topics, nap-taker
Female, 51: my sister—soccer mom, bon vivant
Male, 49: my brother-in-law—paleoanthropologist, beard-tugger
Male, 38: the author—humorist, mangina fearer
Male, 17: my nephew—eleventh-grader, dude
Female, 14: my niece—eighth-grader, jock

The proceedings were as follows: discussion, followed by voting.

DISCUSSION

RARE PERSON WHO NIBBLES GLASS CUPS

Male, 38: What did you think?
Female, 14: Weird.
Female, 72: Very weird.
Female, 51: I felt a little bit sick to my stomach.
Male, 38: And that made it harder for you to enjoy his work, I imagine.
Female, 51: Yeah. I was reminded of every single chipped glass I've ever gotten in a restaurant.
Male, 38: Glasses that he only *started* eating . . .
Male, 49: Look, this whole website is made up. It's an experiment in promotion. But how can you promote nothing? This guy doesn't even exist. It's a test to see how gullible we are.
Male, 72: I had difficulty with this guy, too. His site says you can hire him for a function, but I don't know what kind of function you'd hire him for.
Female, 72: I know exactly: the annual meeting of the Ladies Auxiliary of the West Brookfield Congregational Church. Had the organizer of the event only known

Female, 51: about this guy, she would have hired him. Instead she had a former Miss Massachusetts, who came out in pasties for a hootchie-cootchie act.
Female, 51: I could also see him working as the cleanup guy at a wedding. Or for a very wealthy party-thrower—he could just eat the dishes.
Male, 17: Nice.
Female, 51: The Tiffany Glass company never wants to see this guy coming.

HOT SKATING GRANDMA

Female, 72: I identified with this one. Spunky. A cross between Dr. Ruth and Sonja Hiney.
Female, 51: Dr. Ruth *on* her hiney.
Male, 49: This gal is helping to create a long-term future for skaters. She extends the life of skating.
Male, 38: Yes, she's a positive role model for the skater of a certain age.
Female, 51: The drape of the skirt made by "Karen Santoro, Seamstress for Performers" is very flattering for the older skater: it covers the withers.
Male, 38: Yes, and we're grateful for that. What did you think of the part of the site called "Maria's Closet," where you can click and drag different outfits onto the outline of her body?
Female, 72: You could have a lot of fun putting her bra on her knees.
Male, 38: That *does* sound like fun.
Female, 51: I also love that she has a pinup calendar. Who would order it, though?
Male, 49: I think a lot of gentlemen would buy that calendar.
Female, 72: You think so?

Male, 49: I'm quite sure.
Female, 51: Will, can you imagine buying the calendar?
Male, 72: No.

DANGEROUS BARBECUER GEORGE GOBLE

Female, 72: I wonder what he does with all the time he saves.
Male, 17: Eats.
Male, 38: Was anyone concerned that this site promotes arson? I ask because some of you seemed concerned about the glass eater.
Female, 51: Well, we can all get at glasses. Liquid oxygen is harder.
Male, 72: I think this bit about "One briquette soaked in LOX is approximately equivalent to one stick of dynamite" is similar to when, during Prohibition, you'd see a write-up that read, "You don't want to make alcohol, so *never* mix so many pounds of grain with so many pounds of sugar . . ."
Female, 51: ". . . and *never* let it sit in the closet . . ."
Male, 72: Exactly. It's a subliminal ad for people interested in making car bombs.
Female, 51: Could be. Do you think his wife is sitting home thinking, "Well, at least he's not out gambling . . ."?

PENIS ENTHUSIAST DONNA ANDERSON

Female, 72: I didn't like that one.
Female, 51: Me either.
Male, 49: But, hey—it's there.
Female, 72: It made me feel uncomfortable.
Female, 51: Find a different group to talk about it with. I have my children here.

Male, 72: I had no interest in her.
Male, 38: Okay, so I'm sensing there's a lotta love in the room, a lotta love.
Female, 14: I thought she was hilarious.
Male, 38: And what some people might find refreshing about her, of course, is that, in treating men the way that women have been treated for centuries, she's turning the tables.
Female, 72: That didn't fascinate me.
Male, 49: We can talk about this one later in the locker room.

TOOL PIG

Female, 51: Fun. Needs a better thesaurus.
Male, 38: Too much "beefy"?
Female, 51: Yeah.
Male, 38: His work does provide a service, though. That's a plus.
Female, 51: Mm-hmm. I loved when he said that his tape measure is bulky and might contribute to carpenter's crack.
Male, 38: Now, unlike the glass nibbler or the rabbi or Hot Skating Grandma or the barbecuer or Koko, we don't know what this guy looks like. Is that a disadvantage for him?
Male, 72: I didn't think so.
Male, 38: What do you think he looks like?
Male, 72: Beefy.

ASK THE RABBI

Male, 17: I like him.
Female, 51: Me, too. A defender of the American way. When

	you first read it, you think, "This sounds absurd." But then you realize he has a justifiable position. I loved the letter to Mr. Tapper.
Male, 38:	"Your presence in Canada is a comfort to us all."
Male, 72:	I would like to ask the rabbi, what really got him interested in guns? Was he looking for a novel way to do circumcisions?
Male, 38:	Bris with a bang!
Male, 72:	Exactly.
Male, 38:	I love his picture, too. He's adorable. Which doesn't in and of itself make him funnier, but it does make me like him more, which in turn might make him seem funnier.
Female, 72:	Cute is good. Cute is always good.

KOKO THE GORILLA

Female, 51:	Loved it.
Female, 14:	Really funny.
Female, 51:	I could do the same experiment with my dog. I could get just as good language out of my dog as they're getting out of this gorilla. Maybe even better, because our dog can say hello.
Female, 72:	Koko reminds me of those animal acts on talk shows who refuse to do the act once the cameras are rolling.
Female, 51:	At first I wondered if Koko had Tourette's, and then I wondered if the trainer is kooky. A lot of blurting.
Female, 72:	Nipple!
Male, 38:	And the nice thing about Koko's act is she leaves us wanting more.
Male, 49:	Yes, because it'd be fun to see her make the occasional *appropriate* response.

KUSHAMI ROOM SNEEZE FETISHIST

Female, 72: Odd.
Female, 51: I mean, *I* like to sneeze, too, but . . .
Male, 72: This guy should get into a corelationship with a pepper company.
Female, 72: I was confused by the images of the people on the cold commercial. Does this guy direct the commercials?
Male, 38: No, he just tapes them. He likes to watch.
Female, 72: Okay.
Female, 51: Some of these pictures don't really say "pre-sneeze" to me.
Male, 38: A valid point.

AOLIZA

Male, 17: Pretty cool.
Female, 72: Yes, I identified with this one. This is the same conversation we have every day at the senior center.
Female, 51: And the program worked!
Male, 17: They believed it was a real person.
Female, 51: And they divulged all this information.
Male, 38: Which some might see as an invasion of privacy.
Female, 72: "Does talking about this bother you?"
Male, 38: Liza might be a nice companion for shut-ins.
Female, 72: Or really for anyone with a lot of time on his hands.
Male, 38: Ex-presidents.

VOTING

Each judge was instructed to pick his three favorite entries and to spread a total of ten points over these three selections.
A hush fell over the room.

The judges sighed, scribbled, crossed out.

Some six minutes later, all scoresheets were collected, and I started to tally them up.

The irony was not lost on me: just a month or two earlier our nation had been all but immobilized by the discombobulation surrounding the voting for our president.

—

"Ladies and gentleman," I announced shortly thereafter, "I am pleased to announce that the funniest person on the Internet is a young lady named ....
....
....
....
....
....
....
....
....
....
....
....
....
....
....
....
....
....
....
....
....
....
....
....
....

". . . Koko the Gorilla!"

A cheer went up.

"Not Liza?" my mother asked.

"No, not Liza."

"Oh."

"I thought it might be Liza, too," my nephew added.

I looked at them both apologetically. "Does talking about this bother you?"

—

In the spirit of full disclosure, I will now reveal the specifics of the voting.

The numbers were as follows:

Koko the Gorilla	24
AOLiza	19
Donna Anderson	8
Ask the Rabbi	7
Rare Person	6
Kushami Room host	5
George Goble	1

All hail the chimp.

Nipple.

Love eat.

Drink!

Chapter 18

My official duties are behind me now.

I sometimes think back on that period of my life—that period when I often felt like I was leasing my retinas to the comedy gods—and I shudder. I shudder to think of what I've seen.

I have seen a very thorough analysis of the geographical distribution, as to color, of emergency exit signs across the country (they are mostly red, it seems).

I have seen an ad for a company that allows you to superimpose a photograph of your child's face onto a cloth doll called "Brightness the Clown."

I have seen a site whose copy includes the information "Being a veterinary technician for the past ten years of my life has greatly influenced my artwork, but my empathy for animals is most apparent in the latest body of work I have produced, the Mummification series."

I have read the auction listing, placed by a prisoner on Texas's death row, of the five seats for witnesses to his own execution.

It is possible that some or all of these things would exist even if the Internet did not. But just as likely, some of them—or other items equally as puzzling and disturbing—are a product of the Internet's opening the bilge of our collective unconscious.

Where has the Internet gotten us? I'd like to be able to tell you that it has led to a national health-care system, to electronic voting, to fewer lonely people, to better readers.

I remain cautious.

That said, however, it certainly has made certain kinds of commerce and communication faster, easier, cheaper. And, what is perhaps more important for someone like me, the openness that it has engendered has made for some very interesting viewing. I can't argue with that. Recently, while in an elevator with only one other person, the person sneezed forcibly and loudly, suddenly immobilizing me. Even my *watch* stopped ticking.

—

Think of the end of our search, then, as being the diametric opposite of the last scene of the original *Planet of the Apes*. The craggy, cliff-lined beach of that movie's ending has been replaced by a bar in a Washington, D.C., hotel made famous by adulterous politicians. Our protagonist is not a terrorized outcast in a burlap shift, but a sneery postmodern humorist-voyeur who is capturing the whole scene with his tape recorder.

There's buried treasure in this version, too. But it's not the Statue of Liberty, it's an ape.

Acknowledgments

Kudos once again to Jonathon Karp, who not only edited but also came up with the idea this time. Is Karp slowly edging me out of the authorial equation? Caution must be paid.

Thanks, too, to Jess Taylor, who provided textual embellishment and guidance, and to Laura Peterson, Success's handmaiden.

Random House's Janelle Duryea, Mary Bahr, Beth Pearson, Amelia Zalcman, Sarah McKinney, Laura Moreland, Ed Cohen, Greg Durham, Jim Lambert: you kids put the ZING in publishzing!

A tip of my hat to all—but particularly Adrienne Donald, Sandra Tsing Loh and Mike Miller, Riza Cruz, Peter Terzian, Caleb Crain, Tim Carvell, John Moe, and Michael J. Rosen—who submitted names. Your computers are the Schwab's drugstores of tomorrow.

I beam affection to my focus group members—Ann Earley, William P. Earley, Kendy Madden, Rick Madden, Clay Madden, Annie Madden—so professional in demeanor, yet so unpaid in salary.

Due to strained relations with, not to say a difficult breakup with, one of the aforementioned, this book was written during a trying time in my life. Several people threw into my slough of despond important flotation devices. Larry Norman, Aimée Bell and David Kamp, and Mary South: you are loved.

Web Resources Directory

Websites in Out There
    Abuzz
        [www.abuzz.com]
    Amish.Net
        [www.amish.net]
    Anger Central
        [www.angry.net]
    AOLiza
        [http://fury.com/aoliza]
    Ask the Rabbi
        [www.jpfo.org/askrabbi.htm]
    ChildCare Action Project
        [www.capalert.com]
    Donna's Domain
        [www.metal-sludge.com/DonnasDomain.htm]
    George Goble
        [http://ghg.ecn.purdue.edu/]
    Grammar Lady
        [www.grammarlady.com]
    Harper's Magazine
        [www.harpers.org]
    Hot Skating Grandma
        [www.hotskatinggrandma.com]
    Ironminds
        [www.ironminds.com]
    Jack Swersie
        [www.jackswersie.com]

Jayskids.com
   [www.jayskids.com]
Koko the Gorilla—The Gorilla Foundation
   [www.gorilla.org]
Kushami Room
   [www5a.biglobe.ne.jp/~kago-usu/KushamiRoom/kushami-E.html]
Lin Yin Cai
   [www.linyc.com/linyc/lyce.htm]
Mahir
   [www.members.nbci.com/_XMCM/primall/mahir/081199.html]
Mathemusician
   [www.nctm.org/mt/2000/05/songs.html]
Mister Pants
   [www.misterpants.com]
Mulletsgalore.com
   [www.mulletsgalore.com]
Pat Metheny Group
   [www.patmethenygroup.com]
Plotbytes
   [www.schoolbytes.com]
Prince
   [www.love4oneanother.com]
Rubberburner.com race car driver
   [www.rubberburner.com]
Sneezing Men4Men
   [www.angelfire.com/pop/sneezingm4m/home.html]
Super Greg the dj
   [www.supergreg.com]
The US Music Vault Online
   [www.usmusicvault.com]
Virtual Sin
   [www.virtualsin.com]
Yahoo Internet Life
   [www.zdnet.com/yil]

Other Recommended Humor Sites
Modern Humorist
   [www.modernhumorist.com]

McSweeney's
 [www.mcsweeneys.net]
The Onion
 [www.onion.com]
Playboy
 [www.playboy.com]
Flâneur
 [www.flaneur-ny.com]
Selected Works of Matt Neuman
 [www.mattneuman.com]
Cartoonbank.com: *New Yorker* cartoons
 [www.cartoonbank.com]
Hermenaut
 [www.hermenaut.com]
JustMorons.com
 [www.justmorons.com]
James Lileks
 [www.lileks.com]
The Freedonian
 [www.freedonian.com]
Brett Leveridge
 [www.brettnews.com]
GIGAWIT
 [www.gigawit.com]
Net-Wits
 [www.bminteract.com/netwits]
AdCritic.com
 [www.adcritic.com]
Bush or Chimp?
 [www.bushorchimp.com]
Do the George W. Hump
 [www.george-w-dance.homepage.com]
Create-a-fart (fart sound)
 [www.createafart.com/index.asp]
Rectal Foreign Bodies
 [www.well.com/user/cynsa/newbutt.html]
Who Would You Kill? celebrity death game
 [www.whowouldyoukill.com]

The Filthy Critic
[www.bigempire.com/filthy]
The Gallery of "Misused" Quotation Marks
[www.juvalamu.com/qmarks/]
Reverend Jen
[www.revjen.com]
When Falls the Coliseum
[www.wfthecoliseum.com]
Writers' rejection slips
[www.rejectionslips.com]
More rejection slips
[www.rejectioncollection.com]
One man's rejection slips
[www.dangutman.com/pages/rejection.html]
International Gay Rodeo Association
[www.igra.com]
Pop Update
[www.popupdate.com]
Craig Butler
[www.eclectica.org/v5n1/butler.html]
Jesus impersonator
[www.jesus.com]
Peter Pan impersonator
[www.pixyland.org/peterpan]
Christian comedy
[www.primeexample.com]
Fun with Grapes
[www.sci.tamucc.edu/~pmichaud/grape/]
Prank letters
[www.offrampmotel.com/letters.shtml]
Paul's Subway Diary
[www.eserver.org/sparks/sparks22/subway.html]
Disneyland tourist fashion photos with snotty captions
[www.pattywack.com/tpfashions.html]
Guy obsessed with electricity pylons
[http://users.tinyonline.co.uk/bigh/bigh/pylonof.htm]

About the Author

HENRY ALFORD is the author of two works of investigative humor—*Big Kiss: One Actor's Desperate Attempt to Claw His Way to the Top* and *Municipal Bondage: One Man's Anxiety-Producing Adventures in the Big City.* He has been a regular contributor to *The New York Times Magazine* and *Vanity Fair* and a staff writer at *Spy.* He has also written for *The New Yorker, The New York Times* op-ed page, *Harper's Bazaar, eCompany Now, Travel & Leisure, The Village Voice,* and the online versions of *Playboy* and *McSweeney's.*

About AtRandom.com Books

AtRandom.com books are original publications that make their first public appearance in the world as e-books, followed by a trade paperback edition. AtRandom.com books are timely and topical. They exploit new technologies, such as hyperlinks, multimedia enhancements, and sophisticated search functions. Most of all, they are consumer-powered, providing readers with choices about their reading experience.

AtRandom.com books are aimed at highly defined communities of motivated readers who want immediate access to substantive and artful writing on the various subjects that fascinate them.

Our list features literary journalism; fiction; investigative reporting; cultural criticism; short biographies of entertainers, athletes, moguls, and thinkers; examinations of technology and society; and practical advice. Whether written in a spirit of play or rigorous critique, these books possess a vitality and daring that new ways of publishing can aptly serve.

For information about AtRandom.com books and to sign up for our e-newsletters, visit www.atrandom.com.